TIM SEELIG'S
QUICK FIXES
PRESCRIPTIONS FOR EVERY CHORAL CHALLENGE!

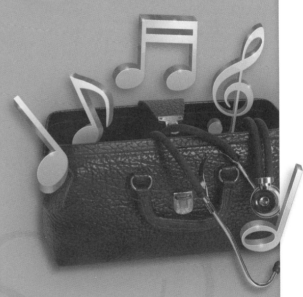

ISBN: 978-1-59235-246-3

www.shawneepress.com

Shawnee Press

Exclusively Distributed By

HAL•LEONARD®
CORPORATION
7777 W. BLUEMOUND RD. P.O. BOX 13819 MILWAUKEE, WI 53213

TABLE OF CONTENTS

IF EXILED ON A DESERT ISLAND AND YOU COULD ONLY TAKE A FEW VOCALIZES FOR EACH AREA OF VOCAL DEVELOPMENT, WHICH ONES WOULD YOU TAKE WITH YOU?

In every area of my life, one of the most difficult concepts for me to grasp is that silly "less is more" thing! It is simply not in my nature. I am a Texan. More is more. Bigger is better. This book, however, is designed to be an easy-to-use handbook, not an all-inclusive tome. I was challenged to select four or five of my very favorite exercises in each of nine categories. Once I began packing, I discovered I just could not do it. I needed more!

I selected my favorite effective exercises that show results. So I organized this resource into groupings that contains six major vocalizes plus four bonuses, totaling around 90! You probably have your own favorites you would like to add!

In each category in this book, you'll find:

1. Six of my favorite exercises with full explanations
2. Four bonus exercises with shorter descriptions
3. A blank page to add your own favorite vocalizes

This handbook will provide you a quick and easy guide with 90 exercises all in one place. So when you are in the middle of a choir rehearsal and you need some help with the sound, you can diagnose the problem and prescribe the quick fix immediately! Definitely the prescription for success!

As choral directors, we are able to diagnose problems as long as we are listening attentively and critically. However, we are not always as good at prescribing how to fix the problems diagnosed. Some clues are visual and some are audible. If we are to make effective changes and maximize the result in a short period of time, we must prescribe concepts that our singers can easily understand and incorporate into singing that will change the sound to produce positive results. Ideally, your musicians will remember the prescription the next time, and every time, they rehearse.

This is not a book of warm-ups that you can study for weeks or days (or minutes) before rehearsal. Up to that point, you hear your chorus only in your mind as you plan for the challenges of a rehearsal.

Here's the scenario. At rehearsal, the choir does the warm-ups you selected. Things go well. But when the ensemble sings the repertoire, all of your careful plans go out the window. They just don't sound like you thought they would. In fact, they don't sound anything like they did during the warm-ups.

THE FIRST TWO SYLLABLES OF THE WORD, REHEARSAL ARE "RE-HEAR."

What do you do?

1. Listen. Listen again. If necessary, ask the singers to repeat the phrase to give you a chance to consider what to do. Remember, the first two syllables of the word, rehearsal are "re-hear."

2. Diagnose the problem quickly.

3. Turn to the correct page to find a quick prescription to address the diagnosed problem.

4. Apply the concept to the problematic area.

5. Smile. You were successful at teaching concepts, not clones.

6. Move on in the music.

7. Repeat as needed.

Although there are countless books on the market with actual musical warm-ups to use with your choir, I've decided NOT to include musical examples in this book for a reason!

While it can sometimes benefit the choir to return to a warm-up from the beginning of rehearsal, it is more effective to stop when a problem is heard. Stop right then and focus on that challenging section of music to determine which choral concept will fix the problem. Most often, singers do not understand the connection between warm-ups and how they apply to the repertoire. By using the choral material they are singing, it allows them to tie them together. Plus, the ensemble is better off to jump right back in with the music where they stopped. They will also retain it better when they sing that section again.

Keep this handbook in your own folder of music. Carry it with you everywhere. Make notes in it. Punch holes and spiral bind it.

Use it often!

If you would like to share your own favorite solutions with other choral directors, send them to me through **www.timseelig.com** where they can be shared with every one!

Timothy Seelig

If some of the names or descriptions seem strange or unfamiliar to you, make sure that you have "THE PERFECT TRIO" in your library. They will answer all your questions!

The Perfect Blend book and DVD
The Perfect Rehearsal book and DVD
The Perfect Choral Workbook and CD ROM

QUICK FIX TIPS - REFERENCE GUIDE

SYMPTOM	QUICK FIX CAN BE FOUND IN CHAPTER

Chapter 1: Posture/Alignment

Lacks Energy	#1
Looks Slouchy	#1
Sings Out of Tune	#1

Chapter 2: Breathing

Sagging Phrases	#2
Lacks Support	#2
Heaving Chests/Shoulders	#2

Chapter 3: Phonation

Tight Sound vs. Breath	#3
Intonation	#3
Production Too Heavy/Forced	#3

Chapter 4: Resonance

Chins Too High	#4
Sound is Too Bright or Too Dark	#4
Spread Sound	#4

Chapter 5: Articulation/Vowels

Vowels Not Matching	#5
Text Not Understandable	#5
No Consonants	#5

Chapter 6: Blend

Screaming in the Top	#6
Tone Quality Not Consistent	#6
Singers Not Listening to Each Other	#6

Chapter 7: Intonation

Intonation	#7
Piano Singing is Lifeless	#7
No Legato	#7

Chapter 8: Communication

Not Making Music	#8
Not Delivering the Text	#8
Not "Engaged"	#8

Chapter 9: Memorization

| Memorization | #9 |

Miscellaneous Quick Fixes

CHAPTER 1

1

HOLDING YOUR INSTRUMENT

Whenever a person begins to play a musical instrument, sport, or hobby, the first thing to learn is how to properly hold the instrument, tool, or equipment to be used.

As conductors, we can make some very dangerous assumptions about the actual "holding" of the vocal instrument. Don't assume everyone knows how to how their instrument. Nothing could be farther from the truth. When playing an instrument, teachers must continually remind the instrumentalist of "form" issues to help them to be successful. Consider how much time athletes spend practicing how to hold a golf club or a tennis racket. And the instruction never stops!

VOCAL ATHLETES

In addition, we do not spend enough time training our singers as vocal athletes. Every athletic activity begins with plenty of time devoted to stretching, starting with the large muscle groups. As choral directors, however, we jump right into our athletic activity using one of the smallest set of muscles in the human body – the vocal folds!

YOU WILL NEVER GET TO THAT "PERFECT" SOUND YOU ARE STRIVING FOR UNTIL EVERY SINGLE CHOIR MEMBER HOLDS HIS OR HER INSTRUMENT PERFECTLY.

PERFECT BLEND

What is perfect blend? It begins with perfect posture from 100% of the singers! We can never be reminded of this enough. If a chorus stands on stage with 80% of the chorus holding their instruments beautifully and 20% slumping or slouching, the audience is sent an immediate and resounding message that the choir really doesn't know what it is doing. You will never get to that "perfect" sound you are striving for until every single choir member holds his or her instrument perfectly.

#1: THE LIST!

Remind your singers often how to correctly hold their vocal instrument. Read this list aloud. Use some of them at every single rehearsal! You can change it up, but don't vary it much.

- Feet = Place feet 6-8 inches apart, one in front of the other.
- Knees = Stand with knees slightly bent.
- Thighs = "Push" thighs down into the floor for grounding.
- Hands = Move hands to side seam of pants or skirt.
- Pelvis = Tuck the pelvis slightly under to elongate the spine.
- Chest = Stand with chest high and expanded.
- Shoulders = Roll shoulders front to back, dropping them back gently.
- Chin = Hold the chin below horizontal.
- Head = Stand erect with no tension (ideally relaxed like a bobble head).
- Eyes = Eyes appear bright and smiling.
- Mind = Engage the mind.

Lastly, imagine standing two inches taller than you think you are.

PRACTICE GOOD HABITS!

#2: COUNTDOWN TO PERFECT POSTURE

Ask your singers to return their bodies to the posture they brought with them to rehearsal. Encourage them to slump, throw one hip out, allow their chests to sag, etc. On the count of three, instruct them, "Hold your instrument for singing!"

Practice good posture over and over. As the chorus becomes accustomed to this exercise, hopefully they will remember many points from the above list. Create habits so the singers pay attention to every detail of how to hold their vocal instrument every time they sing. Repeat this exercise often!

Counting:

1. Slump (similar to a Raggedy Ann or Andy doll).
2. Get ready.
3. Count to three
4. Move into perfect singing position on three.

#3: HUG/ROW

In our daily lives, we constantly slump our shoulders forward. This is caused by using a computer, driving, playing video games, texting, or simply holding music while singing! We must return our singers to a posture that may feel unnatural for them with the shoulders dropped back and the chest elevated.

    1. Hug yourself.
    2. Row back as is rowing a boat.
    3. Repeat.
    4. Drop the arms to the side.

#4: CORNER PRESS

Recently, I underwent physical therapy for my shoulders (imagine that ... a conductor having shoulder pain?). The therapist provided me with a wonderful exercise. She instructed me to stand in a corner, placing one leg in front of the other and situating my hands on the wall, chest height, on either side of my shoulders. I then stepped into the corner, pressed my shoulders back, expanded my chest, and held that position for 30 seconds. I was absolutely amazed by how difficult it was for me. Singers can do this without a corner! The **Corner Press** reminds them of the importance of freeing the muscles across the sternum and opening up the chest for proper posture.

    1. Stand in a corner (mentally), one foot in front of the other.
    2. Place hands on imaginary walls, chest height, on either side of shoulders.
    3. Step inward and press. (the imaginary walls don't move!)
    4. Hold for 10 seconds.
    5. Release.
    6. Repeat exercise with the other foot forward.
    7. Step back, dropping shoulders back & down, chest up.

#5: STERNUM POWER

One of the issues we deal with is separating the position of the chest from the action of inhalation and exhalation. We are accustomed to raising the chest when we inhale and dropping it upon exhalation. This exercise will reverse that habit.

1. Stand tall, placing one hand on sternum.
2. Collapse over as you exhale all of your breath.
3. Stand tall without inhaling, keeping one hand on sternum.
4. Inhale deeply.
5. Exhale fully while maintaining the high sternum. (The hand/sternum must not lower or sag.)
6. Inhale deeply (low).
7. Repeat.

WHEN YOU FEEL YOUR SINGERS ARE SINGING WITH NO ENERGY, STOP THEM IMMEDIATELY AND ENGAGE THEIR BODIES IN THE PROCESS.

#6: WINDMILLS, JOGGING, AND SIT-UPS, OH MY!

When you feel your singers are singing with no energy, stop them immediately and engage their bodies in the process. If their entire bodies are not engaged in the process, then everything else is for naught! Use "faux" physical exercises to get their blood pumping, as well as to get their attention!

1. Faux jog
2. Faux sit-ups
3. Faux javelin throws
4. Faux bowling
5. Faux windmills: hands on back of their heads and twist
6. Faux jumping jacks
7. Faux under water swimming
8. Faux bend and stretch, reach for the sky!
9. Faux knitting (just kidding)
10. Use your imagination!

℞ HOW TALL ARE YOU?

Stand and place a hand on the top of your head. Slump two inches. Next, keeping your chin down, pull an imaginary string from the top of your head. Drop hands. This bonus exercise will make your singers stand four inches taller!

℞ MASSAGE/KARATE KID

Depending on your circumstances, ask your singers to turn to their right and give the person in front of them a shoulder massage. Instruct them to pay attention to the spine and neck areas. Finish with some light karate chops across the shoulder area. Tell the singers to turn around and repeat the process on the new person standing in front of them.

ENCOURAGE THEM TO THINK ABOUT GOOD POSTURE

℞ SYNCHRONIZED SWIMMING

This exercise is a cross between faux swimming and ballet. Dive upward with hands overhead. As the singers lower their arms to each side, encourage them to think about the beautiful posture of a ballet dancer who is always prepared to perform.

℞ PAT DOWN

In this day and age of air travel, imagine that you are taking the choir on tour and the group is flying to the destination. Upon arrival at security, some of the singers looked a little "shady," causing the TSA to pat you all down!

In this bonus exercise, however, each person pats himself or herself down. Tell them to start at the top of the head and to pat all the way down to the feet (to search for musical contraband)! Search back up and then pat down the back.

Your Favorite Posture Quick Fixes

2

Breath is fuel for singing. It is the gas in your vocal car. Air is cheaper than gas, so fill up often! Remind the chorus how much more air they need for singing than the amount they usually access on a daily basis for normal life. In addition to the "unnatural" requirement of good posture while singing, the effective use of breath is something that is also "unnatural" to our daily lives. We use perhaps only 20% of our lung capacity in an "at rest" breath, while we need perhaps 70% or 80% for singing!

All too often, as choral conductors, we try every possible "fix" to adjust the sound of our chorus, ignoring the most basic fix – the breath! As you know, there is no way your chorus can make a sound anyone will want to hear without ample amounts of air. Vocal folds are activated by air passing through them. Sound is carried to the listener on air. Lack of air will result in short phrases, tight singing and it will certainly affect intonation. Other than that, it is not all that important!

As a choral director, one of the most rewarding things to see in our singers (or actually, not see!) is beautiful breathing technique. We fight clavicular breathing at every turn. We encourage them to use a combination of intercostal and abdominal breathing, creating a system of breathing that functions apart from the concept of thoracic pressure. The greatest testament to your teaching of choral technique is if your singers go home after a rehearsal with their bodies and minds exhausted, yet their voices are fresh, or fresher, than when rehearsal began.

BREATHING

All too often, we compare our breathing mechanism to a balloon that we fill with air. Indeed, if we are not using good posture and accessing all of the muscles of the breath mechanism, it is like a balloon. If you slump and inhale, you have to "close off" the top of the balloon resulting in a glottal attack and a tight sound. On the other hand, if you sit or stand correctly, breathing low with chest elevated, you can inhale without "closing off" the top of the balloon. This is the goal. This way, the vocal folds do not have to function as a valve, but are free to phonate without doing double duty!

As a choral director, one of the most rewarding things to see in our singers is beautiful breathing technique. You can never work on breathing technique too much!

2

#1: FARINELLI

We must assist our singers to increase their vital capacity (amount of air in their lungs) for singing. This exercise, attributed to the castrato, Farinelli, is one of the best to address a multitude of issues including phrasing, legato, etc. Your singers will focus on increasing the amount of air taken in for singing, especially accessing the lower portions of the lungs.

1. Allow hands to hang down along sides of body.
2. Inhale for eight counts, raising arms to shoulder height.
3. Roll shoulders around once.
4. Pant for several seconds.
5. Take in another pint of air.
6. Repeat the last three instructions.
7. Exhale slowly while lowering arms (optional: hiss or sing).
8. Keep the sternum elevated until all breath is gone.

#2: SWIMMING UNDERWATER

Once we have "force-filled" the lower lobes of the lungs (imagine a hard and unused sponge on the side of the sink as it is placed under the water), we want our singers to experience what it feels like to empty the lungs completely and fill them very quickly. The best example they can relate to is swimming underwater for a long time and desperately coming up for air!

1. Dive into the pool.
2. Swim underwater with nice, smooth strokes.
3. Release a little air with each stroke.
4. Keep going. You are half way across the pool.
5. Keep going and get rid of all of your air.
6. Depleted, rise to the surface of the water.
7. Fill your lungs!
8. Exhale, keeping chest elevated.

#3: AIR ELEVATOR

The **Air Elevator** is a fun exercise to remind your singers to breathe low all of the time. One of the most serious problems singers encounter repeatedly is high chest singing or clavicular breathing... because we do this every day of our lives.

1. Place one hand sideways where the lowest ribs attach (this will be the ground floor).
2. Take a high and shallow breath to the fourth floor.
3. Release the breath and return to ground floor.
4. Breathe deeply into the sub-basement (abdomen should be low and deep).
5. Notice the difference in the noise of inhalation.
6. Notice that with the high breath comes a glottal attack.
7. Repeat the exercises.
8. Now sing! Not only will the breath work better, the sound will be remarkably altered.

#4: INNER TUBE

In today's world, the most important and difficult breathing achievement is good posture with an elevated chest and shoulders dropped gently back and down. We live in an age where ultra thin is no longer the norm, when attention to the "inner tube" no longer brings the cry, "I can't do that because I'll look fat!" Fortunately, this is a very good thing for singing.

1. Place your hands on your sides (below ribs, above pelvic bone).
2. Take a deep breath to inflate the inner tube (includes entire mid-section).
3. Exhale on a hiss keeping the inner tube inflated (this delays the retraction of the diaphragm).
4. Repeat.
5. This time, sing a phrase.
6. You can demonstrate the opposite, just for fun, by filling the inner tube and allowing it to deflate immediately upon phonation.

#5: PREP BREATH

I'm sure we all took a conducting class where a professor hammered into our heads that singers should always take the initial preparation breath in the tempo of the piece. All too often, this method simply does not work, setting up more problems than it solves by often causing tension, shallow breath, and lack of focus. Just let it go! Train your singers to take a three or four beat preparation breath before entering. Try this method during interludes, too. The **Prep Breath** exercise reminds the singers of the importance of a relaxed, low breath.

2

1. Ask the accompanist to play a two-measure introduction.
2. Direct the chorus to breathe at the last possible moment in the tempo of the piece. Notice the high breath and glottal attack.
3. Repeat the exercise asking the chorus to breathe for four counts (use the air elevator to the sub-basement).
4. Make them aware how much more prepared they are for the entrance.

The next "quick" breath will be relaxed and low.

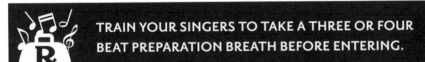

TRAIN YOUR SINGERS TO TAKE A THREE OR FOUR BEAT PREPARATION BREATH BEFORE ENTERING.

#6: CHOO CHOO CH...

After getting the singer's body and big parts of the breathing mechanism in order, it is useful to exercise the flexibility of the epigastrium (the area just below where the rib cage meets). This area must be involved in breathing and the successful execution of most consonants.

1. Place the finger where the lowest ribs meet in the front.
2. Begin by imitating the sound of a slow train, "Choo, choo."
3. Direct the choir to speed up together.
4. Pulse the epigastrium with each "ch" sound.
5. Change to other unvoiced consonants (i.e. K, T, and P).

2

℞ STERNUM POWER AND FARINELLI

Yes, you have already seen these exercises in this book under the posture section. It is an important exercise with many benefits! In this instance, ask the singers to do the exercises as instructed before, but then sing phrases from their repertoire, making sure their sternums stay elevated throughout the exercise.

℞ ITALIAN BREATH

No, *Italian Breath* is not the result of too much garlic! *Italian Breath* is the age-old exercise of blowing out a candle five times in succession paying attention to the movement of the abdomen. I challenge you to reverse the action and suck in five times to replicate the abdominal motion. Muscles are supposed to work in tandem after all. Repeat.

℞ SILENT SIGH

Relax your singers. Have them breathe deeply through their noses. Make sure they are holding their musical instruments well. Now, ask them to take in another deep breath and sigh as they exhale, feeling the movement of the abdomen as the **chests remain elevated**. Repeat. Add any unvoiced consonant such as "s," "sh," "f," or "th."

℞ BREATHE THROUGH A STRAW

We have all heard the instruction, "breathe through a straw." It does work. It slows down the entire breathing process, limits the amount of air entering the lungs, and encourages a low breath. Now, exhale through that same straw. But we cannot always pucker for inhalation. Practice inhalation on every vowel! Use your repertoire as a guide. Select the first vowel of a piece and practice the inhalation.

Your Favorite Breathing Quick Fixes

CHAPTER 3

Every vocal expert reminds us to get out of the way of our own singing, whether or not we really know what that means. The consistent effort is to peel away the tension added over the years. Many of our vocal problems can be solved by this simple exhortation and guidance to let go of our pre-conceived ideas of how the apparatus works. Often, we bring a lifetime of manipulation of our vocal product through a myriad of influences that include aural modeling, parents, friends, teachers, and so on.

SINGING IS COMPLETELY KINESTHETIC AND IT IS BASED ON MUSCLE MEMORY.

In addition, we are unable to actually hear ourselves sing. We "feel" ourselves sing, mostly through bone conduction. So, how would we know what to do, unless a really good vocal technician taught us? Singing is completely kinesthetic and it is based on muscle memory. Your singers only know when something is correct when you tell them and then they have to remember how it felt, not sounded, when you said, "That's it!"

The vocal folds are small (only 1/2"–3/4" in length) and they are so very sensitive. Although small, they vibrate on a wide range of pitches and on a wide range of dynamics – all at a nano-second's bidding. Refer to "The Perfect Blend" DVD (DVD1001) for some killer vocal fold footage!

The major challenge we undertake in learning phonation is to make the laryngeal area as free as possible, using both intrinsic and extrinsic muscles. Our end goal is to not see or experience any tension. We certainly do not want to hear it!

RELATIONSHIP OF BREATH TO PHONATION

Once we have our posture and breathing mechanisms working well, the next issue is all about the relationship of breath to vocal folds – the breath pacing. It is then our choice as to how much air we allow to pass over the vocal folds – from breathy to tight. Hopefully, we are able to find the exact relationship that creates an efficient, but free vocal tone. The messa di voce certainly helps the singer experience the relationship of air to vocal folds. Pulling in on the abdomen abruptly demonstrates a completely different, and mostly detrimental, relationship. With the chest remaining elevated, the abdomen should move in gently – and slowly – as the tone progresses.

#1: THE SCREAM

This exercise has nothing at all to do with screaming. It has to do with easy onset of the vocal tone – resting on the beautiful column of air you have so thoroughly mastered by means of the first two sets of instructions (posture and breathing). What we are trying to do is separate the two functions of the vocal folds: thoracic pressure (lifting weights, etc.) and phonation. Ask your singers to do the following:

1. Sit in a chair in a slumped-over position.
2. Sing a phrase of "America, the Beautiful."
3. Feel the tight onset of tone.
4. Sit tall or stand and hold your instrument correctly.
5. Place your hands on cheeks (scream position).
6. Inhale deeply.
7. Sing the phrase again. Do you feel the dramatic difference in tone quality and freedom of phonation?
8. This can also be done with a simple descending 5-note scale on any vowel.

#2: BLOW YOUR FINGER/BUMBLEBEE

If the sound your singers are producing is tight and does not flow on air, this type of exercise will help correct that problem. You will never get your group to make a unified sound until all of the singers agree on how much air they are using to phonate.

1. Use a portion of the repertoire.
2. Instead of singing with words, sing it while blowing the indexed finger placed in front of the pursed lips.
3. Repeat the exercise again, using the bumblebee lip buzz/trill as notes are sung.
4. Next, sing it on an "oo" vowel using as much air as was used in the previous steps.
5. Finally, sing with the text. Does the group hear the improvement when copious amounts of air are used? Everything will improve including those pesky internal consonants!

#3: BREATH PACING

One of the wonderful concepts used these days is to replace the term, "breath support" with "breath pacing." Given the fact that you have worked diligently to prepare your singers' alignment and breathing functions, you are now ready to adjust the amount of air passing the vocal folds, from tight (hyperfunctional) to breathy (hypofunctional).

1. Take a shallow, inefficient breath.
2. Sing a long phrase, using very little air (Can your choir members name a performer who sings like this?).
3. Next, take a nice deep breath.
4. Sing as much of a phrase as breathy as possible (Again, can the ensemble name a singer who does this?).
5. Finally, ask them to phonate efficiently (the "just right") breath in the middle of tight vs. breathy.

#4: INNER TUBE OCTAVES

Another terrible thing perpetuated in many circles is the sudden jerking in of the abdomen for loud or high notes. This is counterproductive, causing tension, stress, and weight on the vocal folds in an attempt to hold back the onslaught of air and muscle. This is obviously most egregious in high singing.

1. Place your hands on your inner tube.
2. Sing an octave, 1–8–5–3–1, on "ya-ha."
3. First, pull in dramatically on the abdomen muscle for the upper octave. Feel the strain.
4. Next, push out slightly on the inner-tube on the upper notes of the octave.
5. Return to the repertoire, selecting a high entrance or intervallic leap upwards.
6. Repeat.
7. Octaves are everywhere in choral literature. Finding examples to use is easy!

#5: MESSA DI VOCE

Singers often do not know exactly what it takes physiologically to go from soft to loud and back (Messa di Voce). In order to increase dynamics, the instruction from the brain is to increase airflow and, at the same time, increase good tension, adding "mass" to vocal folds to counteract the extra air. The ideal result is a crescendo.

The difficulty is in the decrescendo as the temptation is to cut back on the airflow and to collapse the shape of the resonators.

1. Sing a Messa di Voce on "oo–oh–ah–oh–oo."
2. Experience the natural tendency of the crecendo/decresendo (led by vowels)
3. Sing a Messa di Voce on an "ah" vowel.
4. Experience the physiology required.
5. Move this exercise around throughout the vocal range.
6. Have chorus sing different chords and practice messa di voce on the chord.
7. Find extended crescendos and decrescendos in the repertoire.
8. Have chorus sing an 8-count crescendo and an 8-count decrescendo. (Level 8 is fortissimo - all they have. Level I is pianissimo - with energy.) Ask them to sing a 4. Then a 6 or 2 or 8.
9. Put numbers in your music where you want a level 8 or a 3, etc.

3

#6: MASHED POTATOES VS. SPIN CYCLE

The relationship of the airflow to the vocal fold tension is called **appoggio**, Italian meaning, "to lean." When singers are not focused on free phonation, out of habit they often resort to tight singing. Here's an exercise that will help.

1. Select a chord in the repertoire that sounds tight.
2. Ask the singers to mash an index finger into the palm of their opposite hand as they sing the chord that sounds tight.
3. Next, ask them to gently touch the palm and spin the finger, replicating that feeling with their tone.

Later, when you hear them making the mashed sound, a simple gesture from you will remind them of this spinning concept!

℞ PERSONAL NECK BRACE

Explain to your singers how we miraculously match pitch. The ear, the brain, and the vocal folds do it, not muscles. Place your hands on your neck like a neck brace. Now, play random notes on the piano and ask them to match them as quickly as possible. Use notes that are all over the place. By placing the hands around the neck, this **Personal Neck Brace** reminds them that there should be no tension.

℞ BOWLING BALL TO FEATHER

Sing a chord from the repertoire. Singers should place one hand, palm up at waist level. Ask them to hold an imaginary bowling ball in the other hand, above the up stretched one. They should sing their chord at a fortissimo dynamic as the bowling ball hits the hand. Next, ask them to do the same process with a pretend soft ball, then a ping-pong ball, and finally with an imaginary feather. By practicing the different levels of attack, they experienced the dynamic parameters from fortissimo to pianissimo.

℞ NASCAR

Long before children have any concept of how to drive, they imitate the sound of a car shifting gears. Ask your singers to grab the gearshift knob on the floor of the car. Lead them from first gear through second, third, and fourth gears. Notice how the gears (or in our case, registers) overlap and thin out naturally as they rise. Each gear higher is a higher vocal register. This is a great demonstration of how registers work.

℞ WHAT GOES UP

For everything that goes up, something must counterbalance it in support downwards. Use the octave leap 1–8 on "ya-ha." On the lower pitch, the singers should visualize that they are holding five pound buckets of cement in each hand. For the upper octave, those buckets suddenly weigh fifty pounds. In the same sense, as singers go down in their range, they should "float down" rather than mash or shove.

Your Favorite Phonation Quick Fixes

CHAPTER 4

This is the fun part! Resonance is most often what sets one chorus apart from another. It is in this area that we, as directors, we have the most impact in how we teach concepts and how we model for our choruses. Again, most vocal pedagogs agree that we have unfortunately passed on the phrase "place the tone" to describe this phenomenon that has no basis in reality. To say, "Place the tone in the mask" means nothing to a group of people without someone actually demonstrating the sound.

RESONATOR ADJUSTMENT

4

A much better choice of words is "resonator adjustment." Over the last century, there has been a wide range of resonance adjustment used by choral groups. We really only know about the last century of resonance because of recording archives. Today, we have a wide range of sounds in our choral organizations that run the gamut from the opera chorus on one end to the straight-tone British choral tradition on the other.

Certainly, resonance is driven by repertoire in many respects. However, it is also a matter of conductor's taste. An individual's background, teachers, and exposure to aural modeling have affected these tastes. There are also times when a conductor may not like the sound his or her choir is achieving, but may not know how to change it!

In recent years, we have definitely seen a move toward more "forward" straight-tone singing. Some of this is dictated by the repertoire that is so popular today, including tone clusters that are difficult to tune with vibrato, as well as a move toward more historically authentic representation as we perceive it to be.

RESONANCE AURAL MODELING

One of the biggest issues that plagues us is the fact that we do not listen to singers or speakers who encourage us to replicate good resonance adjustment in our own vocal mechanism. We listen to singers and speakers using a great deal of tweeter on a daily basis. Then, we arrive at rehearsal and need to access that second resonance chamber, the pharynx (throat) that is required for a beautiful, rich tone. This is very difficult. It is our responsibility to listen to and to encourage our singers to listen to music and speakers that we are expecting them to emulate once they arrive at choir rehearsal or performance.

#1: KINDERGARTEN FIX

Music teachers indicating pitch levels with their hands solidifies negative patterns early, unwittingly training singers to reach for high notes with their chins, tiptoes, and all. This is a difficult habit to break, but not impossible.

1. To illustrate the problem, sing an octave scale in a comfortable range from bottom to top and back down.
2. Begin with chin tucked down on the sternum. Move the head up as the pitches rise until the chin is high in the air on the top.
3. As the singers go back down the scale, the chin and head descend.
4. **Reverse the above.**
5. At the bottom of the scale, the head is comfortably thrown back.
6. As the scale ascends, the head angles downward until the chin is almost resting on the sternum for the high note.
7. Reverse this exercise again, head moving up or while singing down the scale.

#2: WOOFERS TWEETERS

To avoid too much discussion about placement, teach "resonator adjustment" instead. *Woofer Tweeters* teaches the singers how to adjust their "tone knobs" from treble to bass on a single pitch.

1. Place a finger in front of mouth, singing a very forward and bright "ah."
2. Move the finger backwards as the resonance moves back adding color to the tone, staying on "ah."
3. Finish with the finger placed behind the ear with a very dark, and even swallowed "ah."
4. Reverse.
5. When you hear a resonance adjustment you want to change, don't use words such as "darken the tone" or "brighten the tone." Show the singers what resonance adjustment you desire by moving your fingers forward or back – adjusting the tone knob!

#3: THE THREE BEARS OF SPACE

The **Three Bears of Space** is one of the most obvious and fun exercises you can do with your singers. Tell them the story of the three bears, demonstrating how each bear would sing a portion of his or her repertoire. I like to use "America, the Beautiful." Stand in three different places. Then, ask the singers to demonstrate each of the three different ways using a section of the repertoire. The choir sings different adjustments according to where you are standing.

> Bear One: Space in the front, vowels in the front. Too bright!
> Bear Two: Space in the back, vowels in the back. Too dark!
> Bear Three: Space in the back, vowels in the front. Just right!

#4: HUMMERS – HIM VS. HUM

Singers constantly struggle with the concept of "chiaroscuro," the balance of light and dark. Our work on resonance adjustment, woofers and tweeters, etc. is something that never goes away as we adjust for different styles of music, different chronological periods, and simply taste.

1. Say "chiaroscuro" (The "ah" is very bright and forward. The "oo" is very round and dark.).
2. Sing your repertoire on "ah."
3. Sing your repertoire on "oo."
4. Hum your repertoire on the word "him."
5. Hum your repertoire on the word "hum."
6. Sing something holding your hand by your mouth as a baby bird wanting to be fed.
7. Repeat, arching the hand at the back of the throat as in a swan shadow puppet.

Do your singers feel the difference? There is not just one "correct" way.

5: THREE BALLOONS

Amateur singers, and sometimes even professional singers, believe the vocal instrument is just that little bump in the front of their neck. The **Three Balloons** exercise helps remind the singers that it is so much more!

1. Hold your hands in a small knot or golf ball in front of the larynx.
2. Sing repertoire with that instrument.
3. Next, hold your hands in a larger circle like a basketball in front of the chest.
4. Sing with that instrument.
5. Finally, drop hands to thigh level as if holding a large beach ball.
6. Sing with that instrument.
7. Never go back to the first example!

#6: FISH LIPS

Fish Lips is a simple exercise to remind singers not to spread their vocal tone all over town. What **Fish Lips** actually does is to elongate the vocal tract, increasing the production of lower overtones as opposed to using "horse teeth" that encourages higher overtones and spread singing.

1. Ask your singers to purse their mouth into "fish lips."
2. Sing your repertoire.
3. Ask the ensemble to sing the phrase with "horse teeth" to illustrate the difference.
4. Most amateur choruses benefit greatly from feeling and hearing the music using "fish lips" versus "horse teeth."

4

(Rx) THIS IS A FAH FAH FINE DAY TODAY

Sing the phrase, "This is a fah fah fine day today" on pitches 1–3–5–8–8–8–5–3–1. Listen. The first "fah" is a natural speech resonance. The second "fah" is what we consider good choral sound. The "fine" is what we would consider a swallowed and dark sound. This exercise is a quick way to get the singers to experience and hear the entire gamut of resonance possibilities.

(Rx) GET RID OF THE NOSE

Singing through the nose rarely results in a pleasant sound (the exception are French vowels). Ask your musicians to sing a very nasal "uh." As they hold the note, ask them to squeeze their nose open and shut several times to hear and feel a timbre change. Next, ask them to sing that same note with a beautiful pear-shaped sound on "ah." Ask them to squeeze their nose open and close again. When the throat is fully open, there should be no change in timbre because of the position of the soft palate.

HAND

Repeat the phrase, "There is no sound that is horizontally conceived that is beautiful" until you believe it! Singing a phrase from the repertoire, ask the singers to raise their entire arm horizontally in front of their face. While singing, indicate they should turn their hands and the sound to a vertical position. Hear the difference?

ELASTIC BAND

Purchase several yards of one-inch wide elastic bands and cut into lengths of 6 inches. This exercise reminds the choir members to sing vertically. Using both hands, stretch the elastic band vertically to the side of where the jaw hinges, to illustrate opening that space. For fun, pull the band horizontally in front of the mouth and ask them to sing in that manner.

Your Favorite Resonance Quick Fixes

4

Although we are in the business of communication, sometimes we forget there must be a connection with the listener. In order to effectively communicate, we must break the text that we are singing down to its smallest parts – the vowels and consonants that create phonemes and syllables and then words and sentences. Before we can jump into the communication that will be addressed in chapter eight, we have to get all of the parts in order first.

IT TAKES WORK TO PRODUCE THE SOUNDS REQUIRED TO ULTIMATELY COMMUNICATE WITH OUR AUDIENCE.

All too often, we sing (and speak) as if we were practicing ventriloquism. It takes work to produce the sounds required to ultimately communicate with our audience. There is nothing easy or natural about it. The old "come canta si parla" (does one sing as one speaks?) may have been true decades ago when people actually spoke in a declamatory style and projected beyond the footlights. However, today, we live in a day of mumbling where a person can talk with a pencil between the lips for a long time without dropping it.

IN ORDER FOR THE ENSEMBLE TO SOUND THE SAME, THEY MUST LOOK AS IF THEY ARE SINGING THE SAME VOWEL!

Have you looked at photos of your chorus members singing and wondered, "Which vowel were they attempting to sing?" You should be concerned if it was a mystery in the photo. In order for the ensemble to sound the same, they must look as if they are singing the same vowel! We also get hung up on the beauty of the vowels (the sound) much to the detriment of the consonants (the noise). Equal time must be given to the proper execution of the consonants. Then, it will all meld into a beautiful whole.

#1: MATCHING VOWELS

Everyone in the chorus must be on the same page regarding vowel production. In **Matching Vowels**, the choir sings the five pure vowels. This exercise is a physical reminder, stolen and adapted from Jo-Michael Scheibe, to demonstrate the dramatic differences in the tone when the group agrees on pure vowels.

- ee – lower chin, round lips, pull it out of the top of your head
- eh – move hand down vertically in front of face for a long, open sound
- ah – loosen the jaw with the hand (insert two fingers in mouth as a reminder)
- oh – "lasso" the lips in a round motion
- oo – pull the tone forward as if singing through a straw (maintain the "ah" space)

90% OF COMMUNICATION IS IN INTENT! HOWEVER, THE 10% THAT LIES IN DEVELOPING THE DETAILS IS HUGE!

#2: MEOW

Did you know there is one word in the English language that includes all of the pure vowels? It is true. Say the word "meow." Say it several times, slowing it way down each time. As you say it or sing it, you can do all of the gestures suggested above in exercise #1, demonstrates the pure form of each vowel, shows the migration from one vowel into the next, and what physiological actions must take place to form the various vowels.

1. Sing "meow" quickly.
2. Sing it very slowly using the five pure vowel sounds listed above in exercise #1.
3. Cue the singers as they arrive on a pure vowel you are desiring.
4. Apply this warm-up to the repertoire.

#3: ISOLATE

Determine which pure vowel you are listening for that you are not hearing. Can you describe to the singers what they are doing wrong and how to improve upon the vowel?

1. Sing entire song or phrase on one vowel.
2. Isolate the problem by singing on the vowels only (no consonants). These are the vowels in the words of the piece. This will help your musicians identify the pure form of the vowels apart from all colloquialisms and dialects.
3. It may help to have them speak or sing the spectrum of vowels:
   Beet, bit, bait, bet, bat, by, balm, bottom, bawl, boat, book, boot

#4: VENTRILOQUISM

Ventriloquism in choral singing is not very entertaining nor does it result in good choral technique or encourage understandability! All too often, our singers may look as if they were practicing ventriloquism, complete with a dummy by their side (just kidding).

1. Hold up a hand as if holding a puppet.
2. Sing a phrase without moving your lips, but rather allowing the "puppet" hand to move.
3. Put away the puppet hand.
4. Sing the phrase again. Use your own lips to articulate the consonants and vowels, even over articulating.
5. Have singers sing a phrase with a pencil in their lips.
6. Take out the pencil and exaggerate vowel formation.

REHEARSALS MUST BE EXAGGERATED IN ORDER FOR YOUR SINGERS TO ACTUALLY REPLICATE IT IN FRONT OF AN AUDIENCE DURING A PERFORMANCE.

#5: CONSONANTS SUBSTITUTION

By now, the chorus has sung the repertoire using only vowels (no consonants). Next, you have to add the consonants back in as punctuation in the glorious legato line the ensemble created. However, the phrases are still not crisp and clear. Select a phrase from your repertoire and try the following:

1. Sing a phrase.
2. Substitute all consonants with "T."
3. Substitute all consonants with "K."

Pick any consonant for the substitution; especially focusing on the consonants the ensemble has difficulty projecting.

#6: CONSONANT DYNAMICS

There are three placements for consonants: initial, medial, final. Each placement presents its own challenges. It becomes complicated to place consonants at the same dynamic level as the vowels surrounding them. I recommend working consonants by performing Ernst Toch's "Geographical Fugue." Beyond that suggestion, however, it is up to you!

1. Select a consonant, such as "K."
2. Select words that have that specific consonant in all three positions and all three dynamic levels (i.e. sing "call" *p*, *mf*, *ff*; sing "taking" *p*, *mf*, *ff*; sing "talk" *p*, *mf*, *ff*)
3. Make sure singers are connecting their bodies to the production of consonants by encouraging them to place a finger on the epigastrium and feeling it pulse when consonants are well produced.

Do the same process on all consonants. Use your imagination. For example, you could use "cake," "kicker," or "cacophony."

Bonus Articulation / Vowel Exercises

5

℞ MOUTHING WORDS

First, mouth the words of the song silently as if someone is reading lips. Next, say the words in a stage whisper. One of the most important things for **Mouthing Words** is the use of breath to propel consonants forward. The stage whisper can help with this. Finally, sing the music with the same articulation, energy, and motion used in the first two steps.

℞ VOWEL FINGERS

There are a couple of simple ways that singers can use their fingers as a reminder for good vowel formation. The first exercise is a simple "ah" with two fingers. The "ah" vowel will find its most natural production with two fingers inserted between the front teeth. Singers also need a constant reminder of lip formation of the "oh" vowel. "Oh" should ideally be formed with the lips wrapped around one finger. In fact, a finger inserted in an "oh" vowel should almost block the sound completely.

℞ LOOSE TONGUE

In this warm-up, loosen all of the muscles of the face. Make different faces alternating silly and scary, scrunching and releasing. Stick out the tongue as far as it will go. Do some rapid tongue movement exercises by simply repeating them as quickly as possible (examples can include "La," "Da," "Ta," or "Na"). Switch consonants and vowels often.

℞ FREEZE FRAME

Videotape your chorus often in rehearsals or performances. Select some "choice" moments to freeze-frame for your singers. Ask them to identify the vowel they are singing. **Freeze Frame** will be a very telling activity.

YOU CAN ALSO ASK IF THEY COULD TELL IF THE SONG THEY WERE PERFORMING WAS HAPPY OR SAD FROM THE FACIAL EXPRESSIONS!

Your Favorite Articulation/ Vowel Quick Fixes

One of the silliest things conductors can say to a chorus is "I want you to sound like one voice." This is silly because they never take the next step to tell the singers which or which one. Those singers who already tend to "stick out" are pretty sure you mean them and will no doubt sing louder. Those who you wish would sing out more to help create a blend, are quite certain you are not referring to them, so they sing even quieter. This only heightens the disparity between singers.

What is blend, anyway? Well, I always begin with the statement, "Blend begins with posture." This raises some eyebrows. However, from the very moment a chorus enters, you can tell if they will have good blend because they look like they know what they are about to do and are eager to carry it out!

Only once we have all of the building blocks presented in the first five chapters of this book, can we move on to make some beautiful choral sounds. Of course, the most important thing you can do is listen. The most important thing your singers can do is to listen to each other.

Use as many exercises as necessary so the singers can listen to each other – not to judge – but to teach what it is they might improve upon themselves.

BLEND PHILOSOPHY

There are two distinct philosophies in choral singing today. One is to get rid of all unique qualities of the human voice to make a chorus sound like one voice. This philosophy is hugely detrimental, if not damaging to the development of the voice. The other philosophy is that every singer should come to the choral singing process with 100% of his or her unique vocal quality and it is our responsibility to craft those singers into a "whole."

Now we have all struggled with that one singer who really does not fit into the choral sound. I usually take that singer aside and in a manner that makes him feel very, very special, I let him know that because of the unique and wonderful quality of his voice, I need him to give perhaps 90% or even 80% of his unique, individual quality. I make sure he knows this is because he is wonderfully unique, rather than less qualified. These singers always feel great and are most often willing to pull back a little bit. The fact that "that" singer doesn't blend most often has to do with either tight phonation or a resonance adjustment that does not match (too bright). If it has to do with a wide vibrato that you can drive a truck through, then bless you!

OF COURSE, THE MOST IMPORTANT THING YOU CAN DO IS LISTEN. THE MOST IMPORTANT THING YOUR SINGERS CAN DO IS TO LISTEN TO EACH OTHER.

#1: ONE VOICE

Most often, the sound you have in your head for each piece of music stays there. We describe it and define it to a point, but it is still some ideological goal to the singers. For each piece in the program that represents a particular style or musical period, do the following:

1. Select a quartet of singers that match the desired sound.
2. Work with them in advance.
3. Ask them to demonstrate a portion of the piece for the full group.
4. Ask the full ensemble to sing that portion and match the quartet's sound. (Light bulbs will go off around the room as the group imitates the sound).

#2: MATCHED PEARLS

In solo singing, it is often stated that a singer, in pursuit of ultimate communication, must make some "ugly" sounds so the listener can appreciate the "beautiful" sounds (Maria Callas comes to mind as someone "who sacrificed everything" for communication...).

In choral singing, we are likely to attempt to make all of the sounds beautiful – like a strand of perfectly matched pearls – without a rock (or a Baroque pearl) in the bunch.

1. Sing a descending five-note scale on one vowel.
2. Insist on consistency of vowel color and freedom of tone (resulting in vibrato).
3. Hold one hand out – palm up.
4. On the final note, use the other hand to pick the tone up as if picking something out of the palm of your hand. This will help the final note stay on the upper edge of the pitch. Some people call this "pulling a tissue out of the box" on the final note.
5. Repeat the five-note descending scale allowing the hand to float up from beside the throat to the sky.

#3: INSTANT CLINIC

Few choruses have the time or the money to bring in expert clinicians to critique what they are doing. And often a clinician will undo some of our efforts simply because he or she listens for different things. Teach your choir how to listen critically for the things you are teaching them! Do an *Instant Clinic*!

1. Stand in a circle and sing the piece.
2. Divide the circle in half. The first half sings for the other half.
3. Allow constructive comments.
4. Sing again and point out successful changes.
5. During a rehearsal in the performance facility, ask half of the choir to stand in the performance space and the other half to sit as audience members. Repeat.

 LET YOUR CHORUS BE THEIR OWN CLINICIAN.

#4: BEAUTY BOX

Every singer on earth has a point beyond which his or her vocal tone suffers (it's called "ugly"). Unfortunately, this is not something you can determine for the chorus as a whole as it involves strict individual evaluation. I call it singing within their "beauty box." Always save something!

1. Sing a climactic portion of a piece.
2. Ask singers to go well beyond their beauty box.
3. When they have maxed out, ask them for more.
4. Evaluate the levels.
5. Sing it again.
6. This time as you ask for more volume, ask them to visualize moving toward that imaginary line, always remaining one step or one inch behind it for that final "push."
7. Use the edge of the beauty box judiciously. Level 8 on the messa di voce scale should only happen a few times each concert.

#5: CHORAL PYRAMID

The ideal building of sound is in the shape of a pyramid, built from the bottom up (not the other way around)! All too often, we end up with an upside down pyramid where the top over balances the bottom. In order to help the chorus be more conscious of this dilemma, begin by singing one part at a time. Continue adding one part at a time asking if everyone can hear every part. It does not always have to build from the bottom up. You can mix and match so that the singers in each section "feel" where the dynamic level for their part should be, since they cannot actually hear themselves.

1. Sing a chord.
2. Separate the parts.
3. Build from the bottom up. Each voice part needs to have slightly less volume than the one below it.
4. Build from the top down. The lower parts "feel" what kind of support they must give to the upper parts.
5. Divide the parts to "feel" the same appropriate relationship.

"CARESS ME WITH YOUR TONE. DON'T ASSAULT ME!"

#6: PATH TO LEGATO

Singing legato depends on a well-developed sense of vowels flowing into one another. We have all kinds of instructions on how to achieve this (i.e. peeling the onion of vowels one layer at a time, etc.). One of the difficulties is that the choir members bring so many different perceptions of speech patterns to each song, regardless of which language is used.

The following three steps will fix almost all legato challenges:

1. Sing entire song or phrase on one vowel.
2. Sing entire song or phrase on written vowels (no consonants).
3. Add in the consonants as punctuation to the vowels.

℞ PULSATING LEGATO

Creating vibrato in singers who do not naturally have it or subconsciously resist it is a constant challenge to vocal teachers or conductors. Straight tone is unfortunately being encouraged in choral singing to the detriment of healthy vocal production. To rectify this, focus on the breath mechanism and freedom of phonation. Sing a five-note descending staccato exercise, bouncing from the epigastrium on "ah." Now, do the same exercise, still bouncing, but sing legato. Allow the final held note to find its own freedom and natural vibrato.

℞ VOWEL MIGRATION

For every tone higher, the instrument requires more space to resonate. The choice of where to find that space is crucial and it must be conscious and directed. Certainly finding that space in the front of the mouth or "tweeter" is not going to produce a beautiful tone. Move toward the closed vowels in most cases. On the "ah" vowel, move toward either "aw" or even "uh" to help create the extra space in the top.

℞ INTERNAL TACTUS

Often, simply keeping the group together in a tempo you have set is a huge challenge. There are many ways to create an inner tactus without having the chorus tap their toes! I strongly discourage the conductor to either clap or, God forbid, snap fingers. Ask the choir members to lightly tap the tempo on their heart with their right hand or pinch their forefinger and thumb to play imaginary finger cymbals to keep the tempo regular.

℞ GET YOUR GROOVE ON

We have frightened our singers into becoming statues! Nothing could be more detrimental to singing than rigidity of the body. Use every trick in your book to get the singers to move, to use their bodies, and to experience a free flow of music throughout their entire being.

Your Favorite Blend
Quick Fixes

6

CHAPTER 7

One of the most interesting issues we deal with as choral conductors is intonation. There are a million tricks in the arsenal that deal with this problem. Just as the major task of the conductor is to listen carefully and constantly, the same challenge is true for each singer. All too often, vocalists operate on autopilot, concerned with all of the other details required to sing and to sing together. We forget one of the most important details is listening! Not only is it the singer's task to remember how singing feels, but also how his or her voice fits in a group.

In every instance, I shy away from physical tricks, such as raising eyebrows, when working on intonation. I find some singers can still sing horribly flat even with their eyebrows elevated all the way to the back of their heads! Intonation problems are mostly issues of listening, not resonance adjustment. All too often, we do not really understand intonation issues, so we automatically default to brightening the vowel. Well ... singers can still sing flat with some bright vowels, too.

INTONATION PROBLEMS ARE MOSTLY ISSUES OF LISTENING NOT RESONANCE ADJUSTMENT.

Finally, we are encouraged by some camps to straighten the tone in effort to find the perfect tuning. However, **straight tone is a vocal fault**. So, the result is singers raising their eyebrows, singing very bright vowels, using straight tone, and all of it out of tune!

As I said earlier in this section, the major issue we have to deal with is listening. Therefore, the following exercises challenge your singers to LISTEN! As a bonus, I've included hints on how to keep the space and energy in pianissimo singing and create an energized legato.

CHALLENGE YOUR SINGERS TO LISTEN!

#1: PICK A DIFFERENT NOTE!

We ask our singers to sing chords. Most often, we tell them which note to sing in the demonstrated chord. Even if we play a chord and ask them to "pick a note" in that chord, they tend to migrate to the notes we habitually dictate to them.

    1. Play a chord.
    2. Pick a note and sing it.
    3. Select a different note in that chord to sing.
    4. Select a third note they have not yet sung.

You will be surprised at the singers' reactions. The first reaction may be "I don't know another note in that chord!" The result is that all of the singers have to think and listen in order to find a note in the sung chord.

#2: SING A DIFFERENT PART

When we are challenged with tuning, it is often an interesting exercise to ask the singers to swap parts. You'll teach several lessons by asking each of the sections to sing someone else's part. Most importantly, they will learn to listen for the other parts more intelligently. Ultimately, your chorus will be able to tune more efficiently.

    1. Select a phrase in the repertoire.
    2. Ask each section to switch and sing a different part.
    3. Return to their designated part.
    4. Hear the difference?

It does not hurt your singers to sing a different part in one song. Certainly, we do not want to require singers to sing over an extended time outside of their comfortable tessitura. However, on one song, it does not hurt at all and it will be beneficial to the final result!

7

#3: SPACIOUS PIANISSIMO

Our singers have the perception that singing softly, or pianissimo, is easy. As choral conductors, we know better. Anyone can sing loudly and as you know, most will. Mastering the art of pianissimo is much more challenging. The greatest danger is that the singers will psychologically "pack up their bags and go home" when they sing softly.

1. On an "ah," sing I–5–I fortissimo and then pianissimo.
2. Listen to what happens to the tone while singing pianissimo.
3. Repeat the exercise making sure the pianissimo singing has the same space and energy as the fortissimo.
4. Move it up and down the range.
5. Apply this exercise to your repertoire.

#4: TRACTOR PULL

This is one of my all-time favorite exercises. *Tractor Pull* teaches beautiful legato and energy in the soft singing.

1. Sing a phrase very choppy and with no sense of legato.
2. Divide the chorus into partners.
3. Ask the pair to grasp each other's wrists in a firm hold.
4. Instruct the partners to find firm footing, step back, and prepare to pull the partner.
5. While pulling firmly, the choir sings the phrase again, singing as the sensation feels.
6. Tell the singers to stop and turn toward you again.
7. Repeat the phrase, instructing the choir to sing it in a choppy manner first. Halfway through, demonstrate a pulling gesture and ask them to replicate the feeling and sound as when they were pulling on their partner.
8. Finally, ask them to pull twice as hard and since twice as softly.

The desired result should be an energetic pianissimo.

#5: LITTLE BUNNY FOO-FOO

Choral guru Rodney Eichenberger reminds us "What they see is what you get." This is seldom more true than while conducting pianissimo. All too often, we encourage our singers to produce tiny, squeezed sounds because those are the gestures we conduct. Exercises #3 and #4 on page 46 can also help remedy this problem.

1. Direct a section while leaning over and making small Bunny Foo-Foo conducting motions while the choir sings a pianissimo phrase in the music.
2. Allow the singers to laugh! They have probably seen Bunny Foo-Foo before from you!
3. Now, stand up tall and ask the chorus to sing the same pianissimo phrase, using the feelings from the muscle memory developed in the above **Tractor Pull** and **Spacious Pianissimo** exercises.

#6: CRESCENDO

In the Messa di Voce, the crescendo is the easiest part. We understand it because we do it more often than a decrescendo. The problem with the crescendo on a climactic portion of a piece is that we lose support of the body and tend to "sing toward the back wall." Both of these reasons can ruin the tone quality of the sound.

1. Sing either a final or a climactic chord.
2. Crescendo, moving the resonance adjustment toward "tweeter" (too bright).
3. Crescendo, moving the resonance adjustment toward "woofer" (fills the space).
4. Place hands on the posterior.
5. Next, crescendo pushing down on the posterior into the thighs and knees (supports the tone).

7

Bonus Intonation Exercises

℞ SING IN A DIFFERENT KEY!

Is the chorus singing out of tune? Trick them by asking them sing a half step higher (warn your accompanist before!). Often moving the singers into a registration that is somewhat higher will encourage them to "take some weight off" of the vocal production and enable them to tune. When you allow them to return to the original key, make sure they replicate the registration from the half step higher. Try it a whole step higher if you dare!

YOU CAN ONLY SING AS BEAUTIFUL A TONE AS YOU CAN IMAGINE OR THINK.

℞ IT IS NOT A SOLO

Listen as you sing! Don't forget that the first two syllables of rehearsal are "re-hear." If any of the singers stop listening to everything that is going on around them, everything will go awry. Ask your singers if they can you hear every other part. If they cannot hear each part clearly, either they are singing too loudly or the seating configuration may need adjusting. If this is the case, ask them move around and sing in quartets.

℞ THINK BEFORE YOU LEAP

You can only sing as beautiful a tone as you can imagine or think. Take the time to create the tone color you want for a particular piece. Make sure you have done sufficient aural modeling so that the singers know the sound you have in your head that you are hoping they will create with their voices. Train them to hear and even emulate that sound in their minds' ears before they ever utter the first tone.

℞ CHANGE RESONANCE PATTERNS

If the chorus still is singing out of tune, change up the resonance patterns on them. Have them hum on "him." Ask them to sing the entire section on a bright "ee." Have them experience the music on all manner of vowels in order to identify whether or not resonance is truly a factor in the intonation challenges they are experiencing.

7

Your Favorite Intonation Quick Fixes

7

CHAPTER 8

If we were not interested in communicating with our audience then why not just play an instrument? We have chosen an art form with communication at its very core. As choral conductors, we have actually combined the art of music and the art of theater into what we are attempting. We strive for perfection in the choral art and forget that the bottom line is whether it reaches or touches the audience. If it does not, then ask yourself why are we doing it? If we do not reach beyond the footlights with our musical message, then it is completely self-serving, even it if is perfect. That, in my view, is pointless.

WE HAVE CHOSEN AN ART FORM WITH COMMUNICATION AT ITS VERY CORE.

This leads us to some inner work with ourselves and our choruses. We must delve into the corporate psyche of the group in several ways. As leaders, we must first determine what is the mission of the group? Why are they singing? Why are they singing for you? What music can we select that will motivate them to work hard, as well as to enjoy the process? How do we keep choral art alive and relevant in a world that is moving at a pace that is much, much quicker than we as choral musicians can keep pace?

The next step is to determine who is your audience. Is your audience full of just friends and family who have to attend? Does the audience include a wider group of people that are interested, not because they have a relative singing, but also because they are curious about choral music and the way it is performed?

Make sure that there is a free channel of communication between you and the singers. Then there is the importance of communication among the singers to consider. If they don't get along with each other, how can they come together to create a unified sound? Finally, there is the ultimate step of communication between the singers and the audience – through you, of course.

"WHY ARE WE SINGING THIS PIECE?"

#1: HONESTY IS THE BEST POLICY

There are times when we simply have not communicated to the singers what might be obvious to us, "Why are we singing this piece?" If you hit a brick wall trying to engage your singers with a piece of music, perhaps you haven't shared the reason you selected it, where it fits in the program, and what you hope to achieve – either with them or the audience – by performing it.

1. Stop the insanity!
2. Tell your choir why you selected the piece.
3. Be open, honest, and vulnerable.
4. Ask them their feelings about the piece and what might help them to understand your position.
5. Now, ask the choir sing it again.

If it still does not work, be willing to let it go!

#2: SYLLABIC EMPHASIFICATION

I know *emphasification* is not a word, I wanted to frighten my editors and spellcheck. It is a good word, though. All too often, one of the detriments to communicating the text is that we do not put the proper emphasis on the proper syllable as discussed in the next exercise.

1. Pick a note in a chord.
2. Sing the ABC's in a legato manner.
3. As you conduct, stress each alternating letter (i.e. **A**, B, **C**, D, **E**, etc.).
4. Sing it again.
5. Pick a phrase in a song. Ask singers to emphasize certain syllables as they did the alternating letters in the alphabet.

This exercise illustrates how you will direct to communicate stressed and unstressed syllables to them through your gestures.

8

#3: RED DOTS

At the very beginning of the musical learning process, give attention to the reality that sung text must mirror spoken text in many ways or it will never be intelligible to the listening audience. Dress rehearsal is too late to bring this up.

1. Mark your own music with a red dot over the syllables you want the singers to emphasize.
2. Ask the singers to do the same in their music.
3. Sing the music with emphasis on the syllables with the red dots.
4. Make sure what you hear is what you wanted.
5. Never allow them to slack off on this part of the learning process.

#4: EMOTIONAL LINE

Most people agree that communication begins and pretty much ends with intent. The first priority of singers is to truly want to communicate with their audience. Halfway between the singers and the audience is an emotional line where they will meet. If the singers over emote (laughing, crying, etc.), the audience will pull way from that line. If the singers under emote (hiding behind music folders), the audience will pull back from that line. The two will never meet and a connection to communicate will not happen.

1. Imagine the line where you will meet and commune (communicate) with the audience.
2. Practice stepping over that line. (Example: During a sad piece, ask the vocalists to visualize someone or something they have lost to connect with that deep emotion.)
3. Practice staying far back from the line. Unfortunately, this is too easy for most choral singers. Can your choir members sense when they have successfully stepped up to the line?

HALFWAY BETWEEN THE SINGERS AND THE AUDIENCE IS AN EMOTIONAL LINE WHERE THEY WILL MEET.

#5: STOP! READ THE TEXT!

When you and your singers are lost in the music (notes, rhythms, dynamics, memory, etc.), take time to revisit one of the first tasks you hopefully did at the very beginning of the concert preparation – read the text.

1. Ask for a volunteer to simply read the text a loud.
2. Now tell someone to read the text as if to kindergartners.
3. Next, ask someone to read the text as theatrical oration.
4. Finally, divide it up. Split the choir into two halves and allow each half to read a sentence at a time.

This allows the singers to hear multiple interpretations to give ideas of how to bring the text to life.

QUESTION YOURSELF AND THE GROUP WHETHER OR NOT THE TEXT WILL BE UNDERSTOOD BY AN AUDIENCE.

#6: MYSTERY GUEST

We might think the chorus is delivering the text well. However, we know the words already! We are the ones who taught them how to create the text. It sits right in front of us. Question yourself and the group whether or not the text will be understood by an audience.

1. Invite one or more "strangers" to rehearsal.
2. Sing a piece from your repertoire for them.
3. At the end, ask them to determine what percentage of the words they understood.
4. Sing it again.
5. Ask them to raise a hand or mark a score every time they do not understand a word.
6. Determine why the text was not understood. Was it a vowel, consonant, syllable, or intent?
7. Sing it again.
8. Now what is the percentage of understood lyrics? 100%, I hope!

8

℞ LONG NOTES HAVE THREE CHOICES!

While we get into the habit of emphasizing every syllable, we forget to pay attention to held notes. We are not midi-files that simply sit still. There are three choices for every held note:

I. Get louder.

2. Get softer.

3. Spin with energy and blossom.

Practice all three choices. Decide which of the three you want on every held note in the music.

℞ VIDEO DOES NOT LIE

Film the group singing several songs of differing styles. Get out the popcorn, turn off the sound, and turn on the video. Challenge your singers to watch facial expressions to determine which song is being sung and what emotion is supposedly being portrayed. Film the group performing again. Ask them to "act" the part of three different choirs:

Choir A: overacting

Choir B: emoting as they think is appropriate

Choir C: deadpan

Watch the whole video back with the three reactions. Not only will the choir enjoy the differences, but they will remember this exercise and the reactions!

℞ BIPOLAR

We sing music that runs the gamut from the silly, tongue-in-cheek, and humorous to the complete opposite end of the spectrum with stately requiems. An amusing exercise taken from acting class is to sing a song with the complete opposite emotion then the intended from the actual words. After a guffaw, return to the real meaning.

℞ NO VIDEO?

All is not lost if you are not able to film your choir. While the use of the video mentioned above is certainly ideal, this exercise can work by dividing the chorus into two groups (regardless of how small the ensemble may be). Have one group perform for the other. Ask them to do the same directives as above, but emote in opposites. Let each section constructively critique the other half's performance.

8

Your Favorite Communication Quick Fixes

CHAPTER 9

The first three books I penned are filled with reasons why choruses should memorize their music. I have heard all of the excuses. And, they are just that – excuses! There are exceptions, of course, such as large symphony choruses or the performance of major works, especially in a foreign language. Frankly, in my opinion, not memorizing just boils down to laziness. There is a fairly exhaustive article on memorization on my website that I recommend to you: www.TimSeelig.com.

If you do nothing else as a conductor, ask your chorus to memorize one song. After they do, most likely they will want to memorize more. Not only will you have more control, but your choir will feel better about it. In addition, the audience loves to hear choruses sing without the barrier of a music folder between them.

Finally, there is no ideal posture while holding a folder full of music. Physiologically, it is simply impossible. It does not matter how many times you have reminded them, how hard they work at it, or how much you protest, your singers will eventually drop their shoulders forward as they hold their music, crushing all hopes for a high sternum, thereby inhibiting the entire breathing mechanism.

RESEARCH SHOWS THAT MEMORIZING MUSIC ACTUALLY AIDS IN THE NEUROLOGICAL HEALTH OF HUMANS AS WE AGE!

So, get on board and give memorization a try (regardless of what your college professor had to say about it. He or she most likely did not put communication with the audience as the first priority of a choral concert). Those of us out in the "real world" of school, church, and community choruses should absolutely make it our first goal. Memorization is one of the greatest keys to success in those arenas.

9